THE BPD ODYSSEY

EMBRACING HOPE AND HEALING
IN BPD

DAVID ACUSTA

Copyright

Copying or reproducing this book without the author's permission is prohibited (© 2024).

Table of Contents

INTRODUCTION 5

CHAPTER 1 8
   WHAT IS BORDERLINE PERSONALITY DISORDER? 8
      DEFINING BORDERLINE PERSONALITY DISORDER 9

CHAPTER 2 20
   THE SCIENCE BEHIND BORDERLINE PERSONALITY DISORDER . 20
      THE BIOLOGICAL BASIS OF BPD 21

CHAPTER 3 33
   EMOTIONAL TURBULENCE IN BORDERLINE PERSONALITY DISORDER 33
      UNDERSTANDING EMOTIONAL DYSREGULATION 34

CHAPTER 4 47
   IDENTITY DISTURBANCE AND SELF-PERCEPTION IN BORDERLINE PERSONALITY DISORDER 47
      UNDERSTANDING IDENTITY DISTURBANCE 48

CHAPTER 5 61
   NAVIGATING INTERPERSONAL RELATIONSHIPS WITH BORDERLINE PERSONALITY DISORDER 61
      THE IMPORTANCE OF RELATIONSHIPS IN BPD 62

CHAPTER 6 76

IMPULSIVITY AND RISKY BEHAVIORS IN BORDERLINE PERSONALITY DISORDER 76
DEFINING IMPULSIVITY IN BPD 77

CHAPTER 7 91
CO-OCCURRING DISORDERS IN BORDERLINE PERSONALITY DISORDER 91
UNDERSTANDING CO-OCCURRING DISORDERS 92

CHAPTER 8 107
NAVIGATING RELATIONSHIPS AND INTERPERSONAL DYNAMICS IN BORDERLINE PERSONALITY DISORDER 107
UNDERSTANDING INTERPERSONAL CHALLENGES IN BPD ... 108

CHAPTER 9 122
BREAKING THE STIGMA: UNDERSTANDING AND ADDRESSING THE MISCONCEPTIONS SURROUNDING BORDERLINE PERSONALITY DISORDER 122
THE NATURE OF STIGMA AND ITS EFFECTS 123

CHAPTER 10 137
THE JOURNEY OF RECOVERY IN BORDERLINE PERSONALITY DISORDER: HOPE, HEALING, AND RESILIENCE 137
UNDERSTANDING RECOVERY IN BPD 138

CONCLUSION 152

INTRODUCTION

Borderline Personality Disorder (BPD) is one of the most misunderstood and often stigmatized mental health conditions. Individuals with BPD frequently experience intense emotions, unstable relationships, and a fragile sense of identity, making everyday life feel overwhelming and chaotic. The symptoms of BPD can vary from severe mood swings, feelings of emptiness, and intense fears of abandonment, to impulsive behavior, self-harm, and difficulty maintaining stable interpersonal relationships. Despite its impact, BPD is often misdiagnosed, or its symptoms are mistakenly attributed to other conditions.

This book is an exploration of Borderline Personality Disorder, offering insight into its complex nature and the challenges faced by those who live with it. The goal is to provide a deeper understanding of BPD not just for those who are affected by it directly, but also for their families, friends, and mental health professionals. With greater understanding, we can reduce stigma and foster compassion for those navigating this difficult journey.

In the pages that follow, we will explore the **core symptoms** of BPD, including emotional dysregulation, impulsivity, self-image issues, and the constant fear of abandonment. We will also delve into the **causes** of BPD, examining the complex interplay of genetic, environmental, and trauma-related factors that contribute to its development.

Central to this book is the notion that **recovery is possible**. While BPD presents significant challenges, it is not a life sentence. We will examine the **therapeutic approaches** that have proven to be effective in managing symptoms and helping individuals lead fulfilling lives, with a special focus on **Dialectical Behavior Therapy (DBT)**, one of the most successful treatment modalities for BPD.

Recovery from BPD is not about perfection it is about progress. This book will explore how individuals can cultivate emotional resilience, improve interpersonal relationships, and develop a more stable sense of self. Through treatment, self-awareness, and the support of loved ones, it is possible to move beyond the pain of BPD and build a life of emotional balance and personal fulfillment.

Whether you are someone struggling with BPD, a family member, or a mental health professional, this book aims to offer hope, understanding, and practical insights to guide you through the complexities of Borderline Personality Disorder. Together, we can move past the misconceptions and work toward healing and empowerment.

CHAPTER 1

WHAT IS BORDERLINE PERSONALITY DISORDER?

Borderline Personality Disorder (BPD) is a complex mental health condition characterized by pervasive patterns of instability in emotions, self-image, behavior, and relationships. First formally recognized in the Diagnostic and Statistical Manual of Mental Disorders (DSM-III) in 1980, BPD remains one of the most misunderstood and stigmatized mental health disorders. This chapter provides a comprehensive overview of BPD, delving into its definition, diagnostic criteria, symptoms, prevalence, and the emotional challenges faced by individuals living with this disorder.

DEFINING BORDERLINE PERSONALITY DISORDER

BPD is classified as a personality disorder, a category of mental health conditions characterized by enduring patterns of behavior, cognition, and emotional regulation that deviate significantly from societal norms. These patterns are often inflexible, pervasive, and lead to significant distress or impairment in personal, social, or occupational functioning. Individuals with BPD experience intense emotional pain, fear of abandonment, and difficulty maintaining stable relationships, which can lead to a profound sense of isolation and misunderstanding.

The term "borderline" originated from early psychoanalytic theory, where it was believed to lie on the "borderline" between neurosis and psychosis. While this outdated view no longer reflects current understanding, the name persists, contributing to ongoing misconceptions about the disorder.

DIAGNOSTIC CRITERIA

According to the DSM-5, BPD is diagnosed based on the presence of at least five of the following nine criteria, indicating a pervasive pattern of instability in interpersonal relationships, self-image, and affect, as well as marked impulsivity:

1. Frantic efforts to avoid real or imagined abandonment.
   Individuals with BPD often fear being left alone or rejected, even in the absence of evidence, leading to desperate attempts to maintain connections.

2. A pattern of unstable and intense interpersonal relationships.

Relationships are often characterized by extremes of idealization and devaluation, known as "splitting."

3. Identity disturbance.

A markedly unstable self-image or sense of self, leading to frequent shifts in goals, values, or opinions.

4. Impulsivity in at least two areas that are potentially self-damaging.

Examples include reckless spending, substance abuse, binge eating, or unsafe sexual behavior.

5. Recurrent suicidal behavior, gestures, or threats, or self-mutilating behavior.

Self-harm is often a way of coping with intense emotional pain or feelings of emptiness.

6. Affective instability due to a marked reactivity of mood.

Individuals may experience intense episodic dysphoria, irritability, or anxiety lasting a few hours to a few days.

7. Chronic feelings of emptiness.
A pervasive sense of inner void or lack of fulfillment.

8. Inappropriate, intense anger or difficulty controlling anger.
Frequent outbursts of rage, often disproportionate to the situation, are common.

9. Transient, stress-related paranoid ideation or severe dissociative symptoms.
Under stress, individuals may experience episodes of paranoia or feeling disconnected from reality.

COMMON SYMPTOMS AND CHARACTERISTICS

The symptoms of BPD can vary widely between individuals, both in intensity and frequency. Some may struggle more with emotional regulation, while others face pronounced difficulties in relationships. Key characteristics include:

1. Emotional Instability:
   Individuals with BPD often feel as though they are on an emotional rollercoaster, with mood swings that can be triggered by seemingly minor events. These emotions are intense and disproportionate to the situation, making it difficult to achieve stability.

2. Fear of Abandonment:
   This fear, whether real or imagined, can dominate the lives of individuals with BPD. It may lead to clinginess, manipulation, or withdrawal to avoid perceived rejection.

3. Black-and-White Thinking:

People with BPD often perceive the world in extremes good versus bad, all-or-nothing. This thinking pattern can complicate relationships and decision-making.

4. Impulsivity:
Engaging in risky behaviors can provide temporary relief from emotional distress but often leads to regret and further emotional turmoil.

5. Self-Harm and Suicidality:
Acts of self-harm, such as cutting or burning, are common coping mechanisms for managing overwhelming emotions.

PREVALENCE OF BPD

Borderline Personality Disorder affects approximately 1.6% of the general population, although some studies suggest the prevalence may be as high as 5.9%. It is more frequently diagnosed in women, though emerging evidence suggests that this gender disparity may reflect differences in help-seeking behavior and diagnostic bias, rather than actual prevalence.

BPD is most commonly diagnosed in young adulthood, as symptoms tend to become more apparent during periods of significant stress or life transition. While the condition can persist throughout life, research indicates that many individuals experience a reduction in symptoms over time, especially with appropriate treatment.

MISCONCEPTIONS ABOUT BPD

BPD is often misunderstood and stigmatized, both in the general population and within the mental health community. Common myths include:

1. People with BPD are manipulative or attention-seeking.
   This misconception arises from behaviors like self-harm or dramatic emotional

reactions, which are often misunderstood as deliberate attempts to manipulate others. In reality, these behaviors reflect deep emotional pain and difficulty regulating emotions.

2. BPD is untreatable.
While BPD is challenging, it is not untreatable. Evidence-based therapies such as Dialectical Behavior Therapy (DBT) have been shown to significantly improve symptoms and quality of life.

3. People with BPD are dangerous.
Media portrayals often exaggerate or sensationalize the disorder, leading to a perception of individuals with BPD as unpredictable or violent. In reality, they are more likely to harm themselves than others.

EMOTIONAL CHALLENGES IN BPD

Living with BPD often feels like navigating a storm of conflicting emotions. Emotional dysregulation is a hallmark of the disorder, with individuals experiencing emotions that are not only intense but also difficult to manage. This emotional intensity can make even minor stressors feel overwhelming, leading to reactions that others may perceive as disproportionate or irrational.

For example, a seemingly small comment from a friend might trigger feelings of rejection or worthlessness, resulting in an emotional outburst or withdrawal. These reactions are not deliberate but stem from an inability to regulate the intense emotions triggered by the situation.

This emotional instability can take a toll on self-esteem, relationships, and overall well-being. Many individuals with BPD struggle with chronic feelings of emptiness or self-loathing, which can fuel cycles of self-destructive behavior.

A GLIMPSE INTO LIVED EXPERIENCES

To better understand the challenges faced by individuals with BPD, consider the following vignette:

Emma, a 27-year-old graphic designer, often feels like she's living on the edge of an emotional cliff. On Monday, her boss gave her constructive feedback, which she interpreted as harsh criticism. She spent the rest of the day spiraling into self-doubt, convinced she was about to be fired. By the evening, her mood had shifted to anger, and she lashed out at her partner, accusing him of not supporting her. Hours later, Emma felt overwhelming guilt and apologized profusely, fearing he would leave her.

This example illustrates the intense emotional reactions, fear of abandonment, and interpersonal challenges common in BPD.

Borderline Personality Disorder is a profound and multifaceted condition that impacts nearly every aspect of an individual's life. While the emotional instability, fear of abandonment, and self-image struggles are challenging, understanding these experiences is the first step toward empathy and effective treatment. By breaking down the stigma and exploring the complexities of BPD, this book aims to provide insight, hope, and practical tools for those living with the disorder and their loved ones.

CHAPTER 2

THE SCIENCE BEHIND BORDERLINE PERSONALITY DISORDER

Borderline Personality Disorder (BPD) is a multifaceted condition with roots in biological, psychological, and environmental factors. To understand BPD fully, one must explore the complex interplay of these influences. This chapter delves into the scientific underpinnings of BPD, including its biological basis, the role of genetics, the impact of childhood trauma, and how it differentiates from other personality disorders.

THE BIOLOGICAL BASIS OF BPD

One of the defining features of BPD is emotional dysregulation, which can be traced back to differences in brain structure and function. Neuroimaging studies have identified abnormalities in key brain regions associated with emotion regulation, impulse control, and interpersonal relationships:

- Amygdala: The amygdala, responsible for processing emotions like fear and anger, is often hyperactive in individuals with BPD. This heightened activity can lead to intense emotional responses to stimuli that others might find minor or insignificant.

- Prefrontal Cortex: The prefrontal cortex, which helps regulate emotions and impulses, is frequently underactive in people with BPD. This imbalance between the amygdala and the prefrontal cortex contributes to the emotional volatility characteristic of the disorder.

- Hippocampus: The hippocampus, involved in memory and learning, may also be smaller or less active in those with BPD. This could explain difficulties in forming consistent self-identity and regulating stress responses.

Neurotransmitter systems, particularly serotonin and dopamine, also play a role in BPD. Dysregulation of serotonin, which influences mood and impulse control, may contribute to the impulsivity and mood swings seen in the disorder. Similarly, dopamine dysregulation can affect reward processing, contributing to the high levels of sensitivity and reactivity often observed.

THE ROLE OF GENETICS IN BPD

Genetics contribute significantly to the development of BPD. Studies on heritability estimate that around 40-60% of the variance in BPD traits is attributable to genetic factors. Research involving twins and family members of individuals with BPD supports this genetic predisposition:

- Family Studies: First-degree relatives of individuals with BPD are five times more likely to develop the disorder than those without a family history.

- Twin Studies: Identical twins show higher concordance rates for BPD traits compared to fraternal twins, underscoring the influence of genetic factors.

Specific genes associated with BPD include those involved in serotonin regulation (e.g., **5-HTTLPR**) and stress response systems (e.g., genes related to the hypothalamic-pituitary-adrenal axis). While no single "BPD gene" exists, a combination of genetic vulnerabilities can increase the likelihood of developing the disorder, particularly in the context of environmental stressors.

ENVIRONMENTAL FACTORS AND CHILDHOOD TRAUMA

While genetics lay the groundwork for vulnerability to BPD, environmental factors often act as triggers. Adverse childhood experiences (ACEs) are particularly influential:

- Trauma:
Studies indicate that 30-90% of individuals with BPD report a history of childhood trauma, including physical, emotional, or sexual abuse. These experiences can disrupt the development of healthy emotional regulation and interpersonal skills.

- Neglect:
Emotional neglect, such as the absence of consistent care or validation, can contribute to the development of a fragile sense of self and a pervasive fear of abandonment.

- Unstable Family Environments:
Growing up in chaotic or invalidating households where emotions are dismissed

or punished can exacerbate vulnerabilities to emotional dysregulation.

Trauma affects the brain's development, particularly in areas responsible for emotion regulation and stress response. Chronic exposure to trauma can lead to heightened sensitivity to perceived threats and difficulty trusting others, both hallmark features of BPD.

PSYCHOLOGICAL THEORIES OF BPD DEVELOPMENT

Several psychological frameworks provide insight into the development of BPD:

1. Biosocial Model:
Proposed by psychologist Marsha Linehan, this model suggests that BPD arises from the interaction of biological vulnerability and an invalidating environment. Biological predispositions, such as heightened emotional sensitivity, become problematic

when caregivers dismiss, ignore, or punish emotional expressions, leading to difficulties in self-regulation.

2. Attachment Theory:
Insecure attachment styles, particularly disorganized attachment, are common in individuals with BPD. These attachment patterns often develop in response to inconsistent or abusive caregiving, resulting in a fear of abandonment and difficulty forming stable relationships.

3. Trauma Models:
These suggest that BPD symptoms, such as dissociation and emotional instability, may be adaptive responses to early trauma. Behaviors like self-harm or emotional outbursts can be seen as attempts to cope with overwhelming emotional pain.

DIFFERENTIATING BPD FROM OTHER DISORDERS

BPD shares overlapping features with other mental health conditions, which can complicate diagnosis and treatment. Understanding the distinctions is crucial for accurate diagnosis:

- BPD vs. Bipolar Disorder:
Emotional instability in BPD can resemble the mood swings of bipolar disorder. However, BPD mood shifts are typically triggered by external events and occur rapidly, often within hours. In contrast, bipolar mood episodes last days to weeks and occur independently of situational triggers.

- BPD vs. Complex PTSD (C-PTSD):
Both disorders may involve emotional dysregulation and interpersonal difficulties, especially in the context of trauma. However, BPD includes identity instability, impulsivity, and a pervasive fear of

abandonment, which are less central to C-PTSD.

- BPD vs. Narcissistic Personality Disorder (NPD):

Both disorders involve difficulties with self-image and interpersonal relationships. However, individuals with BPD are more likely to seek connection and fear rejection, while those with NPD may prioritize self-aggrandizement and struggle with empathy.

Understanding these distinctions ensures that individuals receive appropriate treatment tailored to their specific needs.

WHY SOME PEOPLE DEVELOP BPD WHILE OTHERS DO NOT

The development of BPD results from a combination of genetic vulnerability, environmental stressors, and individual coping mechanisms. Even among those exposed to similar risk factors, not everyone develops the disorder. Resilience, social support, and access to effective coping strategies can mitigate the impact of risk factors.

For example, a child with a genetic predisposition to emotional sensitivity may develop BPD if raised in an invalidating environment. However, if the same child has supportive caregivers who validate their emotions and teach effective coping skills, they may not develop the disorder.

THE IMPACT OF BPD ON BRAIN FUNCTION OVER TIME

Recent research suggests that the brain's structure and function may change over the course of the disorder, especially with effective treatment. For instance:

- Neuroplasticity:

Engaging in therapies like Dialectical Behavior Therapy (DBT) can help "rewire" the brain, improving emotion regulation and impulse control.

- Reduction in Symptom Severity: Longitudinal studies indicate that many individuals with BPD experience a natural reduction in symptoms as they age, particularly in impulsive behaviors and emotional instability.

These findings underscore the potential for recovery and growth, even in individuals with severe BPD symptoms.

THE INTERSECTION OF CULTURE AND BPD

Cultural factors influence how BPD symptoms manifest and are perceived. For example:

- Cultural Expectations:

Societal norms about gender, emotion, and relationships can shape how symptoms are expressed and interpreted. For instance, women are more likely to be diagnosed with BPD, possibly due to stereotypes about emotionality and relational behavior.

- Stigma:
In some cultures, mental health conditions carry significant stigma, leading to under diagnosis or misdiagnosis of BPD.

- Access to Care:
Cultural and socioeconomic factors can affect access to evidence-based treatments, further complicating recovery.

Understanding these cultural nuances is essential for providing effective and equitable care.

Borderline Personality Disorder is a deeply complex condition rooted in a combination of biological, genetic, and environmental factors. Neurobiological differences, genetic predispositions, and adverse childhood experiences all contribute to its development, while psychological theories offer valuable frameworks for understanding how these elements interact.

Although the origins of BPD are multifaceted, advancements in neuroscience and psychology have paved the way for greater understanding and more effective treatments. By recognizing the interplay between biology and environment, we can foster compassion and hope for individuals living with BPD, as well as their families and communities.

CHAPTER 3

EMOTIONAL TURBULENCE IN BORDERLINE PERSONALITY DISORDER

Emotional instability, or dysregulation, is the cornerstone of Borderline Personality Disorder (BPD). It underlies many of the disorder's symptoms, including impulsivity, unstable relationships, and identity disturbance. Understanding the nature of emotional turbulence in BPD is essential for grasping the lived experience of individuals with the disorder. This chapter explores emotional dysregulation, its triggers, the underlying mechanisms, and its effects on daily life, supported by real-life examples and strategies to cope with these challenges.

UNDERSTANDING EMOTIONAL DYSREGULATION

Emotional dysregulation refers to the difficulty in managing intense emotions effectively. For individuals with BPD, emotions can feel like uncontrollable storms intense, overwhelming, and often out of proportion to the triggering event. These emotional responses are not fleeting; they linger, making it hard to return to a baseline state of calm.

Key aspects of emotional dysregulation in BPD include:

- Heightened Sensitivity:
People with BPD often feel emotions more deeply than others. A small slight or criticism might evoke feelings of rejection or worthlessness.

- Intense Reactions:

Emotional responses are not only stronger but also harder to control, leading to outbursts of anger, despair, or fear.

- Delayed Recovery:
Once triggered, emotions take longer to subside, prolonging the distress.

For example, an individual with BPD might interpret a friend's delayed text reply as abandonment. This perception triggers intense fear and sadness, which can escalate into anger or self-loathing, disrupting their entire day.

COMMON EMOTIONAL TRIGGERS

People with BPD are highly sensitive to interpersonal dynamics and environmental cues. Some common emotional triggers include:

- Fear of Abandonment:

Situations where a person feels ignored, rejected, or dismissed can provoke profound anxiety and distress.
- Perceived Criticism or Failure:
Feedback or perceived mistakes can lead to shame, self-criticism, or anger.
- Interpersonal Conflict:
Disagreements or misunderstandings can escalate into intense emotional reactions.
- Feelings of Emptiness:
The chronic sense of inner void can amplify distress when left unaddressed.

For instance, Jane, a 28-year-old with BPD, recalls a time when her boyfriend canceled a dinner date due to work. Though his reasoning was valid, Jane felt deeply hurt and convinced herself he was losing interest. Her emotions spiraled into anger and sadness, culminating in a heated argument that strained their relationship.

BIOLOGICAL MECHANISMS OF EMOTIONAL DYSREGULATION

The intense emotions experienced by individuals with BPD are rooted in neurobiological differences:

- Overactive Amygdala:
The amygdala, responsible for processing emotions, is hyperactive in individuals with BPD, making them more prone to intense reactions.
- Underactive Prefrontal Cortex:
The prefrontal cortex, which helps regulate emotions and control impulses, often functions less effectively, leading to difficulty managing emotional outbursts.
- Impaired Connectivity:
Communication between the amygdala and prefrontal cortex is often disrupted, making it harder to "calm down" after an emotional spike.

These biological differences explain why emotional turbulence in BPD feels overwhelming and uncontrollable, even when the person recognizes that their reaction may not align with the situation.

THE ROLE OF EMOTIONAL MEMORY

Individuals with BPD often struggle to separate past emotional experiences from the present. This phenomenon, known as emotional memory, intensifies current emotional responses:

- Intrusive Past Emotions:
Emotional memories from previous experiences of rejection, abuse, or failure resurface during triggering situations, amplifying distress.
- Difficulty Contextualizing Events:
A small disagreement may evoke feelings tied to past trauma, making it hard to assess the current situation objectively.

For example, Mark, a 35-year-old with BPD, finds himself paralyzed by self-doubt whenever his boss critiques his work. This reaction stems from childhood memories of being harshly criticized by his parents, which resurface in professional settings.

EMOTIONAL DYSREGULATION AND IMPULSIVITY

Impulsivity often arises as an immediate response to overwhelming emotions. These impulsive actions serve as coping mechanisms, albeit maladaptive, to alleviate distress:

- Self-Harm: **Acts like cutting or burning can provide temporary relief from emotional pain by creating a physical distraction.**
- Substance Use: **Drugs or alcohol may be used to numb intense emotions.**
- Risky Behaviors: **Reckless driving, unsafe sex, or binge eating can serve as outlets for pent-up emotions.**

While these behaviors provide momentary relief, they often lead to regret, guilt, and further emotional instability, perpetuating a harmful cycle.

EMOTIONAL DYSREGULATION IN RELATIONSHIPS

Emotional turbulence profoundly impacts interpersonal relationships. People with BPD often experience intense love and connection, but these feelings can quickly shift to anger or distrust. This pattern, known as "splitting," results in viewing others as entirely good or entirely bad.

- Idealization and Devaluation:
Relationships may start with intense admiration (idealization) but can turn to resentment or hostility (devaluation) over perceived slights.
- Fear of Rejection:

Constant fear of being abandoned can lead to clinginess or preemptive withdrawal to avoid perceived rejection.
- Conflict Escalation:
Minor disagreements can spiral into heated arguments due to the intensity of emotional responses.

For example, Sarah, a 24-year-old with BPD, idolized her best friend Maria, often calling her "the only person who understands me." However, when Maria forgot to invite Sarah to a group outing, Sarah felt betrayed and lashed out, accusing Maria of being selfish and untrustworthy.

CHRONIC FEELINGS OF EMPTINESS

Many individuals with BPD report a pervasive sense of emptiness, described as a void that no relationship, achievement, or experience can fill. This emptiness can:

- Exacerbate Emotional Turmoil: Feelings of emptiness amplify distress, making minor triggers feel catastrophic.
- Lead to Destructive Behaviors: Efforts to fill the void, such as substance use or impulsive spending, often backfire, deepening the emptiness.

This void is not merely sadness; it reflects a deeper struggle with identity and self-worth, making it a central feature of emotional turbulence in BPD.

THE PSYCHOLOGICAL IMPACT OF EMOTIONAL TURBULENCE

Living with constant emotional instability takes a toll on mental health and self-perception:

- Low Self-Esteem: Frequent emotional episodes may lead individuals to view themselves as "too much" or "broken."

- Isolation: Strained relationships and fear of judgment often result in social withdrawal.
- Chronic Stress: The physiological impact of prolonged emotional distress can contribute to physical health issues, such as fatigue, headaches, or gastrointestinal problems.

For instance, Alex, a 31-year-old with BPD, shared that he avoids social gatherings because he fears his emotions will spiral out of control, leaving him embarrassed or rejected.

COPING WITH EMOTIONAL DYSREGULATION

While emotional turbulence in BPD is challenging, it is not insurmountable. Effective coping strategies and therapies can help individuals manage their emotions more effectively:

- Mindfulness:

Practices like meditation or deep breathing can help individuals stay grounded in the present, reducing the impact of emotional triggers.

- Dialectical Behavior Therapy (DBT):
DBT teaches skills such as emotional regulation, distress tolerance, and interpersonal effectiveness, empowering individuals to navigate emotional challenges.

- Journaling:
Writing down emotions and triggers can provide clarity and a sense of control.

- Grounding Techniques:
Sensory-based exercises, like holding an ice cube or focusing on physical sensations, can distract from overwhelming emotions.

For example, Lisa, a 29-year-old with BPD, found that journaling helped her identify patterns in her emotional reactions, enabling her to address triggers more proactively.

THE PATH TOWARD EMOTIONAL STABILITY

Recovery from emotional dysregulation is a gradual process that involves building self-awareness, practicing new skills, and seeking professional support. Many individuals with BPD find that with time and effort, their emotional reactions become less intense and more manageable.
Key components of recovery include:

- Self-Compassion:
Recognizing that emotional struggles do not define one's worth.
- Support Networks:
Building relationships with empathetic and understanding individuals.
- Therapeutic Interventions:
Regular engagement in therapy to develop and refine coping skills.

Emotional turbulence in BPD is a profound and pervasive challenge, but it is also a key area for growth and healing. Understanding the roots of emotional dysregulation and its impact on daily life provides a foundation for empathy and effective intervention.

CHAPTER 4

IDENTITY DISTURBANCE AND SELF-PERCEPTION IN BORDERLINE PERSONALITY DISORDER

Identity disturbance, or a fragile and inconsistent sense of self, is a core feature of Borderline Personality Disorder (BPD). It manifests in various ways, including feelings of confusion about personal values, goals, and roles, as well as a fluctuating sense of self-worth. For individuals with BPD, the concept of "who am I?" can be elusive, creating profound emotional and psychological challenges. This chapter examines identity disturbance in BPD, exploring its origins, manifestations, and impact on individuals' lives while offering insights into strategies for managing and strengthening self-identity.

UNDERSTANDING IDENTITY DISTURBANCE

At its core, identity disturbance in BPD refers to an unstable or fragmented sense of self. Unlike most people, whose self-perception remains relatively stable across different contexts, individuals with BPD often experience their identity as fluid and inconsistent, influenced heavily by external factors and relationships.

Key characteristics of identity disturbance include:

- Shifting Roles and Values:
Frequent changes in interests, career goals, or personal values, often driven by external pressures or fleeting emotions.

- Self-Perception in Extremes:
Viewing oneself as entirely good or entirely bad, often oscillating between these extremes.

- Dependence on External Validation:

A tendency to define oneself based on others' opinions or approval, leading to vulnerability in interpersonal relationships.
- Feelings of Emptiness:
A pervasive sense of inner void, contributing to the lack of a cohesive self-concept.

For example, Sarah, a 26-year-old with BPD, describes how her sense of self shifts depending on whom she is with. Around friends who love sports, she becomes an avid sports fan; with artistic friends, she immerses herself in painting. These shifts leave her feeling like a chameleon, unsure of whom she truly is.

ORIGINS OF IDENTITY DISTURBANCE IN BPD

Identity disturbance often stems from a combination of biological, psychological, and environmental factors:

- Childhood Trauma and Invalidating Environments:

Many individuals with BPD report experiencing inconsistent or invalidating caregiving during childhood. Environments where emotions were dismissed, or personal achievements went unacknowledged, can hinder the development of a stable self-identity.

For instance, a child whose parents alternated between extreme praise and harsh criticism may struggle to form a consistent self-view. This instability can carry over into adulthood, resulting in an unclear or fragmented identity.

- Biological Vulnerabilities:

Emotional sensitivity and dysregulation common in BPD can make it difficult for individuals to integrate experiences into a coherent sense of self. Without the ability to regulate emotions effectively, minor setbacks or conflicts can lead to disproportionate shifts in self-perception.

- Cultural and Social Factors:
Societal pressures and cultural expectations can exacerbate identity disturbance. For example, societal norms about appearance, success, or gender roles may cause individuals to adopt personas that feel disconnected from their true selves.

MANIFESTATIONS OF IDENTITY DISTURBANCE IN DAILY LIFE

Identity disturbance affects various aspects of life, including personal relationships, career choices, and decision-making. Common manifestations include:

- Frequent Changes in Interests or Goals:
Individuals with BPD may switch career paths, hobbies, or personal aspirations rapidly, often abandoning one pursuit for another without clear reasons.

- Unstable Relationships:

Relationships often serve as mirrors for self-identity. In BPD, the dependence on others for validation can lead to intense and tumultuous relationships, as shifts in self-perception impact how others are viewed.

- Difficulty Making Decisions:

The lack of a stable sense of self can make decision-making overwhelming. Even simple choices, such as what to wear or eat, can become fraught with anxiety and self-doubt.

- Internal Conflict:

Individuals may experience a tug-of-war between conflicting aspects of their identity. For example, someone might simultaneously view themselves as independent yet crave constant reassurance and support.

IDENTITY AND EMOTIONAL DYSREGULATION

Identity disturbance in BPD is closely tied to emotional dysregulation. Emotional highs and lows can drastically alter self-perception, leading to rapid shifts in identity.

- Influence of Emotional States:
  A person might feel confident and capable when experiencing positive emotions but worthless and incompetent during periods of distress.

- Reactivity to Interpersonal Feedback:
  External validation or criticism often has an outsized impact. A single compliment might lead to feelings of self-worth, while a minor criticism can result in self-loathing.

For example, Daniel, a 30-year-old with BPD, recalls how a colleague's praise for his work made him feel like a rising star in his field. However, when his manager later criticized a small error, he spiraled into feelings of inadequacy, questioning his entire career choice.

THE ROLE OF SPLITTING IN IDENTITY DISTURBANCE

Splitting, or viewing people and situations in black-and-white terms, contributes significantly to identity disturbance. This tendency can also apply to self-perception:

- Idealization and Devaluation of Self:
   Individuals may alternate between seeing themselves as highly capable and feeling entirely worthless.

- Impact on Relationships:
   Shifts in self-perception often lead to corresponding shifts in how others are perceived, straining relationships and reinforcing feelings of isolation.

For instance, Maria, a 34-year-old with BPD, often oscillates between seeing herself as a dedicated professional and as a complete failure, depending on her mood and recent interactions at work.

THE IMPACT OF IDENTITY DISTURBANCE ON MENTAL HEALTH

A fragmented sense of self contributes to several mental health challenges, including:

- Low Self-Esteem:
  Constantly questioning one's worth and identity can erode self-confidence, making it difficult to pursue goals or form healthy relationships.

- Chronic Feelings of Emptiness:
  The lack of a stable self-concept often leaves individuals feeling hollow or disconnected, leading to behaviors like substance use or self-harm as attempts to fill the void.

- Heightened Anxiety:
Uncertainty about one's identity can lead to pervasive anxiety, particularly in social or professional settings where individuals feel they must "perform" a particular role.

COPING WITH IDENTITY DISTURBANCE

While identity disturbance is a challenging aspect of BPD, several strategies can help individuals develop a more stable and cohesive sense of self:

- Dialectical Behavior Therapy (DBT):
DBT includes modules on building self-awareness and emotional regulation, which can help individuals explore and solidify their identity.

- Exploring Core Values:
Identifying personal values and priorities can provide a foundation for decision-making and self-concept.

- Practicing Self-Compassion:
   Accepting oneself as a work in progress can reduce the pressure to have a "perfect" or fully defined identity.

- Mindfulness and Grounding:
   Techniques like mindfulness meditation can help individuals focus on the present moment, reducing the influence of past experiences or external pressures on self-perception.

For instance, Emma, a 27-year-old with BPD, found that journaling about her values and goals helped her identify patterns in her decision-making, enabling her to make choices that aligned with her authentic self.

THE ROLE OF SUPPORT SYSTEMS

Support from friends, family, and mental health professionals is crucial for managing identity disturbance. Trusted individuals can provide:

- Validation: **Reinforcing an individual's worth and strengths, even during moments of doubt.**
- Perspective: **Offering objective viewpoints when self-perception becomes distorted.**
- Encouragement: **Supporting efforts to explore and embrace different aspects of one's identity.**

For example, Jake, a 32-year-old with BPD, credits his therapist and close friend for helping him navigate his identity struggles by providing consistent and nonjudgmental support.

THE JOURNEY TOWARD SELF-DISCOVERY

Developing a stable sense of self is a gradual process, often involving periods of trial and error. Key milestones in this journey include:

- Embracing Complexity: Recognizing that identity can be multifaceted and evolving, rather than fixed or binary.
- Focusing on Strengths: Building on positive traits and achievements to create a foundation of self-worth.
- Setting Boundaries: Learning to differentiate between internal values and external influences can help solidify self-identity.

FINDING HOPE IN THE PROCESS

While identity disturbance is a hallmark of BPD, it is not a permanent state. With time, effort, and support, many individuals find greater clarity and stability in their sense of self. Celebrating small victories along the way whether it's sticking to a goal or feeling comfortable expressing one's true self can reinforce progress and provide motivation for continued growth.

Identity disturbance is one of the most challenging and deeply personal aspects of Borderline Personality Disorder. Its impact extends to nearly every area of life, shaping relationships, decisions, and self-perception. However, understanding its roots and manifestations can pave the way for recovery and self-discovery.

Through therapy, self-reflection, and supportive relationships, individuals with BPD can learn to navigate the complexities of identity and build a more cohesive and authentic sense of self. In the next chapter, we will explore how BPD affects interpersonal relationships, highlighting the challenges and opportunities for growth in this critical area of life.

CHAPTER 5

NAVIGATING INTERPERSONAL RELATIONSHIPS WITH BORDERLINE PERSONALITY DISORDER

Interpersonal relationships are deeply affected by Borderline Personality Disorder (BPD). Individuals with BPD often experience intense emotions, fear of abandonment, and difficulties maintaining stable connections with others. While these challenges can strain relationships, understanding their roots and implementing strategies for healthier interactions can significantly improve relational dynamics. This chapter delves into the complexities of interpersonal relationships in BPD, including common patterns, the influence of emotional dysregulation, and practical approaches for fostering healthier connections.

THE IMPORTANCE OF RELATIONSHIPS IN BPD

For individuals with BPD, relationships often serve as both a source of comfort and a trigger for distress. These connections can validate self-worth and provide emotional security, but they can also highlight vulnerabilities, such as fear of rejection or inadequacy.
Key features of relationships in BPD include:

- Intense Emotional Bonds:
Individuals with BPD often feel an overwhelming need for closeness, leading to intense attachments.
- Fear of Abandonment:
A core feature of BPD is a pervasive fear of being abandoned or rejected, which can lead to behaviors aimed at preventing separation.
- Idealization and Devaluation:

Relationships may swing between extreme admiration (idealization) and intense criticism or distrust (devaluation).

For example, Emily, a 27-year-old with BPD, describes her relationships as "all or nothing." She either feels entirely loved and secure or completely rejected and unworthy, with little middle ground.

FEAR OF ABANDONMENT AND ITS IMPACT

Fear of abandonment is one of the most prominent challenges in relationships for individuals with BPD. This fear can be triggered by real or perceived signs of rejection, such as:

- A delayed response to a message.
- A partner expressing a need for personal space.
- Changes in routine or attention.

BEHAVIORS RESULTING FROM FEAR OF ABANDONMENT

- Clinginess:
Constantly seeking reassurance or attention from a partner or friend.
- Testing Relationships:
Engaging in behaviors to see if someone will "prove" their commitment.
- Preemptive Breakups:
Ending relationships out of fear that the other person will leave first.

For instance, Sarah, a 29-year-old with BPD, recalls ending a long-term relationship because she felt her partner was becoming distant. In hindsight, she realized her perception was based on fear rather than reality.

THE ROLE OF EMOTIONAL DYSREGULATION IN RELATIONSHIPS

Emotional dysregulation amplifies the intensity of interpersonal conflicts in BPD. Minor disagreements or misunderstandings can escalate into major conflicts due to heightened emotional sensitivity.

PATTERNS OF EMOTIONAL DYSREGULATION IN RELATIONSHIPS

- Overreaction to Conflict:
A minor argument may provoke feelings of worthlessness, rage, or despair.
- Difficulty Recovering from Emotional Episodes:
After a conflict, it can take longer to return to a calm state, prolonging tension in the relationship.
- Projection of Insecurity:
Individuals with BPD may project their insecurities onto others, believing their partner feels the same way about them as they feel about themselves.

For example, Alex, a 32-year-old with BPD, often interprets his wife's frustration as a sign that she no longer loves him. This leads to defensive or accusatory behavior, further straining their relationship.

SPLITTING IN RELATIONSHIP

Splitting, or viewing people in extremes as either entirely good or entirely bad, is a common relational challenge in BPD. This black-and-white thinking can lead to rapid shifts in feelings toward others.

HOW SPLITTING AFFECTS RELATIONSHIPS

- Idealization:
In the early stages of a relationship, individuals may view their partner as perfect, placing them on a pedestal.
- Devaluation:
If the partner fails to meet expectations, feelings can shift dramatically to frustration

or anger, often accompanied by withdrawal or confrontation.

For instance, Maria, a 25-year-old with BPD, recalls how she idolized her best friend Clara for always being "there for her." However, when Clara canceled plans due to work, Maria felt betrayed and accused her of not caring about their friendship.

IMPULSIVITY AND RELATIONSHIP DYNAMICS

Impulsive behaviors, a hallmark of BPD, can also impact relationships. These behaviors often arise in moments of heightened emotional distress and may include:

- Risky Decisions:
Impulsively ending relationships or engaging in affairs.
- Arguments:
Picking fights over perceived slights.
- Reckless Actions:

Using substances or self-harming to cope with relationship stress.

While these actions provide temporary relief, they often lead to regret and further complicate relationships.

THE PUSH-PULL DYNAMIC IN BPD RELATIONSHIPS

The push-pull dynamic is a recurring pattern in BPD relationships characterized by alternating behaviors of seeking closeness and pushing others away.

- Pulling Closer:
Seeking intimacy, attention, and validation to feel secure.
- Pushing Away: Creating distance due to fear of vulnerability or rejection.

For example, Jason, a 34-year-old with BPD, frequently accuses his partner of not loving him enough but then distances himself when his partner tries to show affection, fearing he will be let down.

THE IMPACT OF BPD ON FRIENDS AND FAMILY

Relationships with friends and family are also affected by BPD. Loved ones often find themselves navigating the emotional highs and lows of the individual with BPD, which can lead to:

- Emotional Exhaustion:
The intensity of interactions may leave friends and family feeling drained.
- Uncertainty:
Loved ones may struggle to predict emotional reactions, creating tension and distance.
- Guilt:
Witnessing the individual's struggles can lead to feelings of helplessness or guilt.

For example, Rachel, whose sister has BPD, shares how she often feels torn between wanting to help and needing to set boundaries for her own well-being.

NAVIGATING ROMANTIC RELATIONSHIPS

Romantic relationships are particularly complex for individuals with BPD. While these relationships provide a sense of connection and security, they are also vulnerable to the challenges discussed above.

STRATEGIES FOR HEALTHIER ROMANTIC RELATIONSHIPS

- Open Communication:
Sharing fears and triggers with a partner can foster understanding and reduce misinterpretations.
- Establishing Boundaries: Both partners should agree on healthy boundaries to

protect the relationship from excessive conflict or dependence.
- Couples Therapy:
Professional guidance can help partners navigate the unique challenges of a BPD relationship.

For instance, Anna and her partner John attended therapy together, which helped them understand Anna's fear of abandonment and develop strategies to address it without escalating conflicts.

BUILDING HEALTHIER RELATIONSHIPS

While relationships can be challenging for individuals with BPD, they are not doomed to fail. With self-awareness, support, and practice, it is possible to cultivate healthier and more stable connections.

PRACTICAL TIPS FOR BUILDING STRONGER RELATIONSHIPS

- Practicing Mindfulness:
Mindfulness exercises can help individuals stay present and reduce overreactions during conflicts.

- Using Dialectical Behavior Therapy (DBT) Skills:
DBT includes modules on interpersonal effectiveness, which teach strategies for healthy communication and boundary-setting.

- Avoiding Assumptions:
Taking time to clarify misunderstandings rather than jumping to conclusions can prevent unnecessary conflicts.

- Prioritizing Self-Care:
Maintaining physical and emotional well-being makes it easier to engage in relationships from a place of strength.

For example, Daniel, a 29-year-old with BPD, learned to use DBT skills like "DEAR MAN" (an acronym for effective communication) to express his needs to his friends without feeling overwhelming guilt or fear of rejection.

THE ROLE OF SUPPORT SYSTEMS

A strong support system can make a significant difference for individuals with BPD. Supportive relationships provide stability, validation, and a safe space to work through emotional challenges.

BUILDING A SUPPORT NETWORK**

- Therapists and Counselors:
Professionals can provide tailored strategies and a nonjudgmental environment for exploring relational patterns.
- Peer Support Groups:
Connecting with others who understand BPD can foster empathy and shared coping techniques.
- Family Education:
Educating loved ones about BPD can improve understanding and reduce tension.

For instance, Clara's family attended a psychoeducation workshop on BPD, which helped them empathize with her struggles and offer support more effectively.

HOPE FOR RELATIONSHIP GROWTH

Despite the challenges, many individuals with BPD develop meaningful and fulfilling relationships. Growth is possible when both the individual and their loved ones are willing to work together to understand and address the dynamics of BPD.

Key steps toward growth include:

- Acknowledging Challenges:
Recognizing the impact of BPD on relationships is the first step toward improvement.
- Commitment to Change:
Consistent effort, including therapy and skill-building, is essential for fostering healthier connections.

- Celebrating Progress:
Small victories, like resolving a conflict calmly or expressing emotions constructively, should be acknowledged and celebrated.

Interpersonal relationships in the context of Borderline Personality Disorder are both a source of deep connection and significant challenge. The emotional intensity and fear of abandonment that characterize BPD can strain relationships, but they also offer opportunities for profound growth and healing.

By understanding the dynamics of BPD relationships and adopting practical strategies for healthier interactions, individuals with BPD and their loved ones can build stronger, more stable connections. In the next chapter, we will explore the role of impulsivity in BPD, examining its impact on decision-making, behavior, and overall well-being.

CHAPTER 6

IMPULSIVITY AND RISKY BEHAVIORS IN BORDERLINE PERSONALITY DISORDER

Impulsivity is one of the most prominent and complex traits associated with Borderline Personality Disorder (BPD). It refers to acting without fully considering the consequences, driven by immediate emotional states or the need for instant gratification. For individuals with BPD, impulsivity can manifest in various ways, such as reckless spending, substance abuse, self-harm, or sudden life-altering decisions. While these behaviors can provide temporary relief from emotional distress, they often lead to regret and negative long-term consequences. This chapter explores the causes, manifestations, and impact of impulsivity in BPD, as well as strategies to mitigate its effects.

DEFINING IMPULSIVITY IN BPD

Impulsivity in BPD is characterized by:

- Acting Without Thinking:
Decisions are made quickly, without fully considering the potential outcomes.
- Emotion-Driven Actions:
Impulsivity is often triggered by intense emotional states, such as anger, sadness, or fear.
- Difficulty Delaying Gratification:
Individuals may struggle to resist temptations or urges, even when delaying would lead to better outcomes.

For example, Kate, a 28-year-old with BPD, describes how she impulsively quit her job after an argument with her supervisor. While the decision temporarily relieved her frustration, it left her struggling financially and emotionally.

THE ROLE OF EMOTIONAL DYSREGULATION IN IMPULSIVITY

Emotional dysregulation a hallmark of BPD plays a significant role in impulsive behavior. Intense emotions can overwhelm an individual's ability to think rationally, leading to quick, often risky actions.

KEY FACTORS LINKING EMOTIONAL DYSREGULATION TO IMPULSIVITY

- Overwhelming Urges:
Strong emotions create a sense of urgency to act, making impulsivity feel unavoidable.
- Difficulty Regulating Responses:
The inability to soothe emotional distress increases the likelihood of impulsive reactions.
- Seeking Immediate Relief:
Impulsive actions often provide short-term emotional relief, reinforcing the behavior.

For instance, Sam, a 30-year-old with BPD, recalls how he frequently turned to gambling after arguments with his partner, using the rush of placing bets to escape feelings of anger and sadness.

MANIFESTATIONS OF IMPULSIVITY IN BPD

Impulsivity in BPD can appear in various aspects of life, including personal relationships, finances, and physical health.

COMMON RISKY BEHAVIORS

1. Reckless Spending:
   - Impulsive purchases or financial decisions that lead to debt or regret.
   - For example, Emily spent her entire paycheck on luxury items after a stressful week, leaving her unable to pay rent.

2. Substance Abuse:

- Using drugs or alcohol to cope with intense emotions or escape reality.
- For instance, Jack started binge drinking after feeling rejected by a friend, which eventually escalated into dependency.

3. Unsafe Sexual Activity:
- Engaging in unprotected or risky sexual encounters without considering the consequences.
- Maria, a 25-year-old with BPD, recalls a pattern of one-night stands during periods of emotional distress, which often led to feelings of shame and regret.

4. Self-Harm or Suicidal Gestures:
- Engaging in self-injurious behaviors, such as cutting, as a way to manage overwhelming emotions.
- While not always impulsive, these acts often occur during moments of intense emotional pain.

5. Aggressive Outbursts:

- Sudden, unprovoked anger directed at others, often damaging relationships.
- For example, Lisa shouted at a coworker over a minor disagreement, leading to disciplinary action at work.

BIOLOGICAL AND PSYCHOLOGICAL ROOTS OF IMPULSIVITY IN BPD

The origins of impulsivity in BPD are multifaceted, involving biological, psychological, and environmental factors.

BIOLOGICAL FACTORS

- Brain Structure and Function:
  Studies suggest that individuals with BPD may have differences in brain regions responsible for impulse control, such as the prefrontal cortex.
- Neurotransmitter Dysregulation:
  Low levels of serotonin a neurotransmitter linked to mood and impulse control may contribute to impulsivity.

PSYCHOLOGICAL FACTORS

- Childhood Trauma:

Early experiences of neglect, abuse, or invalidation can disrupt emotional regulation and impulse control development.

- Attachment Issues:

Insecure attachment patterns may lead to impulsive behaviors as attempts to gain attention or avoid abandonment.

THE CYCLE OF IMPULSIVITY IN BPD

Impulsivity in BPD often occurs in a cyclical pattern:

1. Trigger:

A stressful event or intense emotion acts as a catalyst.

2. Impulsive Action:

The individual engages in a risky behavior to cope with the distress.

3. Temporary Relief:

The behavior provides short-term relief or distraction from the emotional pain.

4. Negative Consequences:

The impulsive action leads to regret, shame, or practical challenges (e.g., financial loss).

5. Increased Emotional Distress:

The negative consequences heighten emotional distress, restarting the cycle.

For example, Chloe, a 29-year-old with BPD, shared how she impulsively ended friendships whenever she felt slighted. While this provided immediate relief from her frustration, it often left her feeling isolated and regretful.

IMPULSIVITY IN RELATIONSHIPS

Impulsivity can significantly impact interpersonal relationships, leading to conflict, mistrust, and instability.

COMMON RELATIONSHIP CHALLENGES LINKED TO IMPULSIVITY

- Sudden Breakups:
Ending relationships impulsively during arguments or emotional episodes.
- Jealousy and Accusations:
Acting on perceived slights or fears without verifying the facts.
- Inconsistent Behavior:
Alternating between clinginess and withdrawal, confusing partners or friends.

For instance, David, a 34-year-old with BPD, frequently accused his partner of infidelity without evidence, leading to repeated arguments and eventual separation.

THE CONSEQUENCES OF IMPULSIVITY

While impulsive behaviors may provide short-term relief, they often have long-term negative consequences, including:

- Financial Instability: Reckless spending or gambling can lead to debt and stress.
- Legal Issues: Impulsive acts, such as shoplifting or reckless driving, may result in legal troubles.
- Health Risks: Substance abuse, unsafe sex, and self-harm increase the risk of physical and mental health complications.
- Damaged Relationships: Impulsive outbursts or actions can erode trust and connection with loved ones.

For example, Jenny, a 31-year-old with BPD, lost her job after impulsively yelling at her boss. The incident strained her financial situation and self-esteem.

MANAGING IMPULSIVITY IN BPD

Despite its challenges, impulsivity in BPD can be managed through therapy, self-awareness, and coping strategies.

THERAPEUTIC APPROACHES

1. Dialectical Behavior Therapy (DBT):
   - DBT is highly effective for managing impulsivity, teaching skills like mindfulness, distress tolerance, and emotion regulation.

2. Cognitive-Behavioral Therapy (CBT):
   - CBT helps individuals identify and change impulsive thought patterns, replacing them with healthier behaviors.

3. Medication:
   - In some cases, mood stabilizers or antidepressants may help reduce impulsivity by addressing underlying emotional dysregulation.

PRACTICAL STRATEGIES

1. Pause and Reflect:
   - Practicing the "STOP" skill (Stop, Take a step back, Observe, Proceed mindfully) can help interrupt impulsive actions.

2. Delay Gratification:
   - Setting a rule to wait 24 hours before making significant decisions can reduce impulsivity.

3. Create a Safety Plan:
   - Having a plan for managing self-harm urges, such as calling a trusted friend or therapist, can provide alternatives to impulsive behaviors.

4. Engage in Healthy Outlets:
   - Channeling energy into exercise, art, or journaling can provide relief without negative consequences.

BUILDING SELF-AWARENESS

Developing self-awareness is crucial for managing impulsivity. By recognizing triggers and patterns, individuals can better anticipate and address impulsive urges.

TOOLS FOR SELF-AWARENESS**

- Journaling:
    - Writing about emotions and behaviors can help identify triggers and patterns over time.
- Mindfulness Practices:
    - Meditation and grounding exercises can increase awareness of the present moment, reducing the likelihood of impulsive reactions.
- Feedback from Others:
    - Trusted friends or therapists can provide insights into impulsive behaviors and their consequences.

HOPE AND RECOVERY

While impulsivity is a challenging aspect of BPD, it is not insurmountable. With the right support and strategies, individuals can learn to manage their impulses and make healthier choices.

SUCCESS STORIES

- Emma's Journey:
After years of impulsive spending and relationship struggles, Emma committed to DBT and developed strategies to manage her urges. Today, she feels more in control and has rebuilt her financial stability.

- Jake's Progress:
Jake used mindfulness and journaling to understand his triggers for substance use. Over time, he replaced drinking with healthier coping mechanisms, improving his relationships and mental health.

Impulsivity in Borderline Personality Disorder is a significant challenge, but it is also an area of immense potential for growth and change. By understanding the roots of impulsivity, recognizing its manifestations, and adopting effective management strategies, individuals with BPD can break free from destructive patterns and lead more balanced, fulfilling lives.

CHAPTER 7

CO-OCCURRING DISORDERS IN BORDERLINE PERSONALITY DISORDER

Borderline Personality Disorder (BPD) rarely exists in isolation. A significant proportion of individuals diagnosed with BPD experience co-occurring mental health conditions, also known as comorbidities. These co-occurring disorders complicate the clinical presentation of BPD, making diagnosis and treatment more challenging. However, understanding the interplay between BPD and its common comorbidities is essential for effective treatment planning and improved outcomes. This chapter explores the most prevalent co-occurring disorders in BPD, their impact on individuals, and strategies for integrated treatment.

UNDERSTANDING CO-OCCURRING DISORDERS

Co-occurring disorders refer to the presence of two or more diagnosable mental health conditions in the same individual. In the context of BPD, these disorders can amplify the core symptoms of BPD, such as emotional dysregulation, impulsivity, and unstable relationships.

WHY ARE CO-OCCURRING DISORDERS COMMON IN BPD?

Several factors contribute to the high rates of comorbidities in BPD:
- Shared Risk Factors:
Genetic predispositions, childhood trauma, and environmental stressors often underlie both BPD and other disorders.
- Emotional Dysregulation:
The heightened emotional sensitivity in BPD makes individuals more susceptible to

developing anxiety, depression, and substance use disorders.
- Diagnostic Overlap:
Some symptoms, such as impulsivity or emotional instability, overlap between BPD and other conditions, leading to dual diagnoses.

COMMON CO-OCCURRING DISORDERS IN BPD**

DEPRESSION AND BPD

Depression is one of the most frequent comorbidities in BPD, affecting nearly 60% of individuals with the disorder.

Symptoms of Depression in BPD:
- Persistent sadness or feelings of emptiness.
- Loss of interest in previously enjoyed activities.
- Fatigue and difficulty concentrating.

Impact on BPD:
Depression exacerbates feelings of hopelessness and worthlessness, intensifying suicidal ideation and self-harming behaviors. The combination of depression and BPD often leads to greater functional impairment and emotional distress.

ANXIETY DISORDERS AND BPD

Anxiety disorders, including generalized anxiety disorder (GAD), panic disorder, and social anxiety disorder, commonly co-occur with BPD.

Symptoms of Anxiety in BPD:
- Excessive worry or fear.
- Physical symptoms such as rapid heartbeat, sweating, and restlessness.
- Avoidance of social situations or perceived threats.

Impact on BPD:

Anxiety magnifies fear of abandonment and interpersonal sensitivity, leading to heightened emotional reactivity in relationships. It also increases the likelihood of impulsive decisions made to alleviate distress.

POST-TRAUMATIC STRESS DISORDER (PTSD) AND BPD

There is significant overlap between BPD and PTSD, particularly among individuals with histories of childhood trauma or abuse.

Symptoms of PTSD in BPD:
- Flashbacks or intrusive memories of traumatic events.
- Hypervigilance and exaggerated startle responses.
- Avoidance of reminders of the trauma.

Impact on BPD:
PTSD symptoms can intensify the emotional instability and impulsivity characteristic of

BPD. Additionally, individuals with both conditions often struggle with trust and intimacy, further complicating interpersonal relationships.

SUBSTANCE USE DISORDERS (SUD) AND BPD

Substance use disorders are prevalent in BPD, with studies estimating that 50–70% of individuals with BPD struggle with addiction.

Patterns of Substance Use in BPD:
- Using substances to cope with emotional pain or numb intense feelings.
- Alternating periods of heavy use and abstinence, often reflecting the instability of BPD.

Impact on BPD:
Substance use can exacerbate impulsivity, impair judgment, and increase the risk of self-harm or suicidal behavior. It also

complicates treatment, as addiction often requires specialized interventions.

EATING DISORDERS AND BPD

Eating disorders, particularly bulimia nervosa and binge eating disorder, frequently co-occur with BPD.

Symptoms of Eating Disorders in BPD:
- Unhealthy relationships with food, such as binging, purging, or extreme dietary restrictions.
- Body image dissatisfaction and low self-esteem.

Impact on BPD:
The dysregulated eating behaviors associated with eating disorders mirror the emotional dysregulation in BPD. These behaviors often serve as maladaptive coping mechanisms for managing distress or achieving a sense of control.

OTHER PERSONALITY DISORDERS AND BPD

BPD may also co-occur with other personality disorders, such as avoidant, dependent, or antisocial personality disorders.

Impact on BPD:
The presence of additional personality disorders can complicate interpersonal dynamics and further hinder emotional regulation.

THE INTERPLAY BETWEEN BPD AND CO-OCCURRING DISORDERS

The interaction between BPD and its comorbidities often creates a "vicious cycle" of worsening symptoms. For example:
- An individual with BPD and depression may feel abandoned by a loved one, leading to a depressive episode. In response, they might engage in impulsive behaviors, such

as substance use, which exacerbates feelings of shame and hopelessness.
- Someone with BPD and PTSD may experience a traumatic flashback, triggering intense emotional dysregulation. This might lead to a self-harming episode, which further reinforces feelings of helplessness.

Understanding these interactions is critical for effective treatment planning, as addressing one condition often impacts the severity of the other.

CHALLENGES IN DIAGNOSING CO-OCCURRING DISORDERS

Accurately diagnosing co-occurring disorders in individuals with BPD can be challenging for several reasons:
- Symptom Overlap:
Many symptoms, such as emotional instability or impulsivity, are common across multiple disorders.
- Diagnostic Bias:

Clinicians may focus on the more apparent symptoms of BPD, overlooking additional conditions.
- Self-Reporting Limitations:
Individuals with BPD may struggle to articulate their experiences clearly, complicating diagnosis.

For example, a patient presenting with chronic feelings of emptiness and irritability may initially be diagnosed with depression. However, upon closer examination, they may also meet the criteria for BPD and an anxiety disorder.

THE IMPACT OF CO-OCCURRING DISORDERS ON TREATMENT

Co-occurring disorders significantly influence the treatment of BPD:

INCREASED COMPLEXITY:

- Addressing multiple conditions requires a tailored, multi-faceted approach.
- For instance, treating BPD alongside substance use disorder requires balancing emotion regulation skills with addiction recovery strategies.

HIGHER TREATMENT RESISTANCE

- Individuals with co-occurring disorders may take longer to respond to therapy or require more intensive interventions.
- For example, a patient with BPD and PTSD might initially struggle with exposure-based therapies due to heightened emotional sensitivity.

ELEVATED RISK OF RELAPSE

- Co-occurring disorders increase the risk of relapse, as improvements in one condition may trigger symptoms in another.

EFFECTIVE TREATMENT APPROACHES FOR CO-OCCURRING DISORDERS IN BPD

Integrated treatment is essential for addressing the complex needs of individuals with BPD and co-occurring disorders.

DIALECTICAL BEHAVIOR THERAPY (DBT)

DBT is highly effective for BPD and can be adapted to address co-occurring conditions like depression, anxiety, and substance use disorders.

Key Components of DBT:
- **Mindfulness:** Enhancing present-moment awareness.
- **Distress Tolerance**: Building skills to manage emotional crises.
- **Emotion Regulation:** Developing healthier ways to cope with intense emotions.
- **Interpersonal Effectiveness:** Improving communication and relationship skills.

TRAUMA-FOCUSED THERAPIES

For individuals with BPD and PTSD, therapies like Eye Movement Desensitization and Reprocessing (EMDR) or Trauma-Focused Cognitive Behavioral Therapy (TF-CBT) can help process and reduce the impact of traumatic memories.

MEDICATION MANAGEMENT

Medications, such as antidepressants, mood stabilizers, or antianxiety drugs, may be used to address specific symptoms of co-occurring disorders. However, medication is often most effective when combined with therapy.

INTEGRATED DUAL DIAGNOSIS TREATMENT (IDDT)

For BPD and substance use disorders, IDDT combines addiction recovery strategies with emotion regulation and coping skills, ensuring both conditions are addressed simultaneously.

THE ROLE OF SUPPORT SYSTEMS IN RECOVERY

Support from family, friends, and peer groups is crucial for individuals managing BPD and co-occurring disorders.

FAMILY PSYCHOEDUCATION

Educating families about BPD and its comorbidities can reduce stigma and improve support dynamics.

PEER SUPPORT GROUPS

Connecting with others who have similar experiences can provide validation, encouragement, and shared coping strategies.

THERAPIST COLLABORATION

Close communication between therapists, psychiatrists, and other healthcare providers ensures a cohesive treatment approach.

HOPE AND RESILIENCE IN CO-OCCURRING DISORDERS

Despite the challenges, recovery is possible for individuals with BPD and co-occurring disorders. Success stories often highlight the importance of perseverance, self-awareness, and a strong support network.

For example, Mia, a 35-year-old with BPD, PTSD, and substance use disorder, initially struggled with therapy. However, through DBT, trauma-focused therapy, and peer support, she gradually developed healthier coping mechanisms and rebuilt her life.

Co-occurring disorders in Borderline Personality Disorder present unique challenges, but they also offer opportunities for growth and healing. By addressing the interconnected nature of these conditions through integrated treatment, individuals with BPD can achieve significant improvements in their mental health and overall quality of life.

CHAPTER 8

NAVIGATING RELATIONSHIPS AND INTERPERSONAL DYNAMICS IN BORDERLINE PERSONALITY DISORDER

Relationships are central to human existence, providing support, companionship, and meaning. However, for individuals with Borderline Personality Disorder (BPD), relationships are often a source of both profound connection and intense distress. BPD is characterized by pervasive difficulties in interpersonal dynamics, stemming from fear of abandonment, emotional dysregulation, and a fluctuating sense of self. These challenges can strain relationships with family, friends, romantic partners, and colleagues.

This chapter explores the unique ways BPD impacts interpersonal relationships, the underlying mechanisms of these dynamics, and strategies for fostering healthier, more stable connections.

UNDERSTANDING INTERPERSONAL CHALLENGES IN BPD

Interpersonal difficulties are one of the core diagnostic criteria for BPD. These challenges often manifest in the form of:
- Fear of Abandonment:
A pervasive fear that loved ones will leave or reject them.
- Intense Emotional Reactions:
Strong emotional responses to perceived slights or conflicts.
- Unstable Relationships:
Patterns of idealization and devaluation in close relationships.

For example, Sarah, a 26-year-old with BPD, recalls her tendency to form deep attachments quickly, only to experience overwhelming anger or sadness when those connections faltered.

KEY FEATURES OF RELATIONSHIP CHALLENGES IN BPD

- Black-and-White Thinking:
Seeing people as entirely good or bad, often switching between these views.
- Dependency:
Relying heavily on others for emotional support, sometimes leading to codependency.
- Conflict and Volatility:
Frequent arguments, misunderstandings, and emotional outbursts.

THE ROLE OF FEAR OF ABANDONMENT

One of the most defining characteristics of BPD is an intense fear of abandonment. This fear often leads to behaviors aimed at preventing perceived or actual loss, such as:

- Clinging:
Seeking constant reassurance or attention.
- Pushing Away:
Preemptively ending relationships to avoid being hurt.
- Testing Boundaries:
Engaging in actions to gauge the loyalty of loved ones.

ORIGINS OF FEAR OF ABANDONMENT

- Early Attachment Issues:
Childhood experiences of neglect, inconsistency, or abuse may create an insecure attachment style.
- Trauma:
Losses or betrayals in early life can heighten sensitivity to abandonment.

For instance, Jake, a 30-year-old with BPD, shares how his fear of being left alone often led him to sabotage his relationships, creating a self-fulfilling prophecy.

PATTERNS OF IDEALIZATION AND DEVALUATION

Many individuals with BPD experience intense, all-consuming connections that quickly shift to feelings of betrayal or anger. This dynamic, known as **splitting**, is rooted in difficulties integrating complex views of others.

CYCLE OF IDEALIZATION AND DEVALUATION

1. Idealization Phase:
   - Viewing someone as perfect or the solution to their emotional struggles.
   - Overwhelming affection and high expectations are common.

2. Triggering Event:
   - A perceived slight, disagreement, or unmet need disrupts the idealization.

3. Devaluation Phase:

- The person is seen as hurtful, untrustworthy, or neglectful.
- Intense anger or withdrawal often follows.

For example, Rachel recalls how she would idolize her friends, feeling they could do no wrong, only to later feel betrayed over minor issues, leading to strained or broken friendships.

EMOTIONAL DYSREGULATION IN RELATIONSHIPS

Emotional dysregulation plays a significant role in the interpersonal difficulties of BPD. Intense emotions, such as anger, sadness, or fear, often drive reactions that others perceive as unpredictable or disproportionate.

COMMON EMOTIONAL RESPONSES IN BPD

- Explosive Anger:

Outbursts during conflicts, often leading to regret.

- Intense Sadness:
Deep despair when relationships feel unstable.

- Anxiety:
Worry over how others perceive them or whether they'll be abandoned.

These emotional responses often result in a cycle of conflict, reconciliation, and further emotional distress.

THE IMPACT OF BPD ON DIFFERENT RELATIONSHIPS

FAMILY RELATIONSHIPS

- Challenges:
Misunderstandings, blame, and emotional volatility can strain family bonds.

- Opportunities:
With education and support, families can become a stabilizing force in recovery.

ROMANTIC RELATIONSHIPS

- Challenges:
Romantic relationships often bear the brunt of BPD symptoms, such as jealousy, dependency, and fear of abandonment.
- Opportunities:
Partners who are empathetic and informed about BPD can help foster stability and growth.

FRIENDSHIPS

- Challenges:
The push-and-pull dynamics of idealization and devaluation can make sustaining long-term friendships difficult.
- Opportunities:
Supportive friends who understand boundaries and emotional needs can provide valuable companionship.

WORKPLACE RELATIONSHIPS

- Challenges:

Misunderstandings and conflicts can arise from emotional reactivity or perceived slights.
- Opportunities:
A structured and supportive workplace can help reduce stress and provide stability.

FOSTERING HEALTHIER INTERPERSONAL DYNAMICS

While BPD poses significant challenges to relationships, individuals can develop skills and strategies to improve their interactions with others.

THERAPEUTIC INTERVENTIONS

1. Dialectical Behavior Therapy (DBT):
   - DBT emphasizes interpersonal effectiveness, teaching skills like assertiveness, active listening, and boundary setting.

- For example, DBT helps individuals express their needs without resorting to manipulation or anger.

2. Cognitive-Behavioral Therapy (CBT):
   - CBT helps reframe negative thought patterns about relationships, promoting healthier perceptions of others.

3. Couples and Family Therapy:
   - Therapy involving loved ones can address misunderstandings, improve communication, and strengthen bonds.

BUILDING SELF-AWARENESS

Developing self-awareness is crucial for recognizing and interrupting destructive patterns in relationships.

Tools for Self-Awareness:
- Journaling to reflect on triggers and reactions.

- Practicing mindfulness to stay grounded during conflicts.
- Seeking feedback from trusted individuals.

ESTABLISHING BOUNDARIES

Healthy relationships require clear boundaries to protect both parties' emotional well-being. For individuals with BPD, setting and respecting boundaries can be particularly challenging.

Strategies for Boundary Setting:
- Clearly communicating personal limits and needs.
- Practicing saying "no" without guilt or fear of rejection.
- Respecting the boundaries of others, even during emotional episodes.

DEVELOPING EMOTIONAL REGULATION SKILLS

Learning to manage intense emotions is essential for maintaining stable relationships.

Techniques for Emotional Regulation:
- Deep breathing or grounding exercises during emotional surges.
- Delaying reactions by stepping away from triggering situations.
- Using DBT skills, such as the "STOP" technique (Stop, Take a step back, Observe, Proceed mindfully).

SUPPORT FOR LOVED ONES OF INDIVIDUALS WITH BPD

Relationships are a two-way street, and the loved ones of individuals with BPD often face their own challenges. Educating and supporting these individuals can improve relational dynamics.

EDUCATION AND EMPATHY

- Understanding the symptoms and triggers of BPD can reduce misunderstandings.
- Empathy for the struggles of the person with BPD fosters compassion and patience.

PRACTICING SELF-CARE

- Loved ones must prioritize their own well-being to avoid burnout.
- Joining support groups or seeking therapy can provide valuable tools and validation.

SETTING REALISTIC EXPECTATIONS

- Recognizing that recovery takes time can help loved ones avoid frustration or resentment.
- Focusing on small improvements rather than perfection fosters hope.

SUCCESS STORIES AND HOPE FOR THE FUTURE

Despite the challenges, many individuals with BPD successfully navigate and improve their relationships. Success often hinges on a combination of therapy, self-awareness, and mutual understanding.

Case Study: Anna and Her Partner
Anna, diagnosed with BPD, and her partner, Mark, faced years of turmoil due to her intense emotional reactions and his difficulty understanding her needs. Through couples therapy and Anna's participation in DBT, they learned to communicate more effectively, establish boundaries, and support each other. Today, their relationship is far more stable and fulfilling.

Relationships are a source of both immense challenges and profound opportunities for growth in individuals with Borderline Personality Disorder. By understanding the unique interpersonal dynamics of BPD and adopting strategies for communication, emotional regulation, and boundary-setting, individuals with BPD and their loved ones can foster healthier, more stable connections.

CHAPTER 9

BREAKING THE STIGMA: UNDERSTANDING AND ADDRESSING THE MISCONCEPTIONS SURROUNDING BORDERLINE PERSONALITY DISORDER

Stigma is one of the most significant challenges faced by individuals with Borderline Personality Disorder (BPD). Despite increased awareness of mental health in recent years, pervasive misconceptions and negative stereotypes about BPD persist, leading to discrimination, isolation, and barriers to effective care. These misconceptions often affect individuals with BPD, their loved ones, and even the professionals tasked with providing treatment.

This chapter delves into the origins of stigma surrounding BPD, its impact on individuals and society, and strategies to challenge and dismantle these prejudices. By promoting education, empathy, and advocacy, we can create a more inclusive and supportive environment for those living with BPD.

THE NATURE OF STIGMA AND ITS EFFECTS

WHAT IS STIGMA?

Stigma refers to negative attitudes, stereotypes, or discriminatory behaviors toward individuals based on their perceived differences. In the context of mental health, stigma often manifests as:

- Public Stigma:
Societal stereotypes and prejudices against those with mental illness.

- Self-Stigma:

Internalized shame or self-blame experienced by individuals with mental health conditions.

- Institutional Stigma:
Systemic barriers, such as inadequate funding for mental health services or discriminatory policies.

THE UNIQUE STIGMA OF BPD

BPD carries a particularly harsh stigma compared to other mental health conditions. Common misconceptions label individuals with BPD as:

- Manipulative or Attention-Seeking:
Misinterpreting their emotional needs and behaviors.

- Difficult to Treat:
Assuming BPD is a hopeless diagnosis.

- Unpredictable or Dangerous:
Amplifying fear and misunderstanding.

These labels are not only inaccurate but deeply harmful, perpetuating cycles of shame and preventing individuals from seeking or receiving proper care.

ORIGINS OF STIGMA SURROUNDING BPD

The stigma associated with BPD stems from several historical, cultural, and systemic factors:

HISTORICAL MISUNDERSTANDINGS

- Misdiagnosis:
For decades, BPD was misunderstood and conflated with other conditions, such as schizophrenia or bipolar disorder. This led to its reputation as a "wastebasket" diagnosis for difficult cases.

- Outdated Theories:
Early theories framed BPD as a character flaw or moral failing rather than a legitimate mental health condition.

MEDIA REPRESENTATIONS

- Films, TV shows, and other media often portray individuals with BPD as unstable, manipulative, or violent, reinforcing harmful stereotypes.
- For example, characters with traits resembling BPD are frequently depicted as dangerous or irrational, perpetuating fear and prejudice.

COMPLEXITY OF SYMPTOMS

- BPD's multifaceted symptoms, such as emotional instability and intense interpersonal dynamics, are often misunderstood by the public and even some
- mental health professionals.

Behaviors like self-harm or impulsivity are misinterpreted as attention-seeking rather than expressions of deep distress.

HEALTHCARE SYSTEM BIASES

- Many healthcare providers view BPD patients as challenging or unresponsive to treatment, contributing to therapeutic nihilism.
- A lack of specialized training in treating personality disorders exacerbates these biases.

THE IMPACT OF STIGMA ON INDIVIDUALS WITH BPD

EMOTIONAL AND PSYCHOLOGICAL EFFECTS

- **Internalized Shame:**
Stigma often leads individuals to blame themselves for their struggles, exacerbating feelings of worthlessness and hopelessness.

- **Social Isolation:**
Fear of judgment may cause individuals to withdraw from relationships or avoid seeking support.

BARRIERS TO TREATMENT

- Delayed Diagnosis:
Many individuals with BPD hesitate to seek help due to stigma, resulting in delayed diagnosis and treatment.

- Ineffective Care:
Stigmatizing attitudes among healthcare providers can result in misdiagnosis, inadequate care, or outright dismissal of patients' concerns.

Negative Self-Perception
Stigma reinforces negative beliefs about oneself, such as being "broken," "unlovable," or "a burden," which can worsen symptoms like depression and anxiety.

For instance, Maria, a 29-year-old with BPD, shares how being labeled as "too emotional" by her peers made her feel alienated, discouraging her from seeking therapy for years.

STIGMA IN PROFESSIONAL SETTINGS

Healthcare providers often play a critical role in perpetuating or dismantling stigma. However, stigma within professional settings remains a significant barrier:

- **Challenges in Clinical Practice Therapeutic Nihilism:**
Some providers view BPD as untreatable, leading to reduced effort or engagement in therapy.

- **Bias Against Emotional Expression:**
Clinicians may misinterpret emotional outbursts or dependency as manipulation, reinforcing negative stereotypes.

- **Lack of Training:**
Many professionals lack sufficient training in treating personality disorders, leading to frustration and misunderstanding.

CONSEQUENCES OF PROFESSIONAL STIGMA

Individuals with BPD may avoid seeking care due to past negative experiences. A lack of trust between patients and providers hinders therapeutic progress.

For example, Ben, a 34-year-old with BPD, recalls being dismissed by an emergency room doctor who referred to him as "attention-seeking" after a self-harm episode, leaving him reluctant to seek help in the future.

ADDRESSING STIGMA THROUGH EDUCATION

Education is one of the most effective tools for combating stigma. By increasing awareness and understanding of BPD, we can challenge misconceptions and promote empathy.

PUBLIC EDUCATION CAMPAIGNS

- **Awareness Initiatives:**
Campaigns highlighting the realities of living with BPD can counteract harmful stereotypes.

- **Storytelling:**
Sharing personal stories of individuals with BPD fosters connection and reduces fear.

SCHOOL AND WORKPLACE TRAINING

- Incorporating mental health education into schools and workplaces can normalize discussions about BPD and other conditions.
- Training programs for teachers and managers can promote early identification and support for individuals struggling with BPD.

MEDIA RESPONSIBILITY

- Encouraging accurate and compassionate portrayals of BPD in media can shift public perceptions.
- Advocacy groups can collaborate with content creators to develop nuanced representations of BPD.

EMPOWERING INDIVIDUALS WITH BPD

Empowering those with BPD to advocate for themselves and challenge stigma is crucial.

1. Building self-awareness
Education about BPD helps individuals understand their condition, reducing self-stigma and fostering self-compassion.

2. Promoting self-advocacy
Encouraging individuals to voice their needs and share their experiences can challenge stereotypes and inspire change.

3. Fostering Peer Support

Connecting with others who have BPD through support groups or online communities provides validation and reduces isolation.

For instance, Sam, a 25-year-old with BPD, joined an advocacy group where he found strength in sharing his story, helping to educate others and combat stigma.

THE ROLE OF ADVOCACY AND POLICY CHANGE

Advocacy plays a pivotal role in addressing systemic stigma and promoting equitable treatment for individuals with BPD.

POLICY ADVOCACY

- Advocating for increased funding for mental health services ensures access to specialized care for BPD.

- Policies that mandate mental health training for healthcare providers can reduce biases and improve treatment outcomes.

COMMUNITY PARTNERSHIPS

Collaborating with schools, workplaces, and community organizations spreads awareness and fosters inclusive environments.

GLOBAL MOVEMENTS

Organizations like the National Alliance on Mental Illness (NAMI) and World Health Organization (WHO) are instrumental in promoting mental health education and reducing stigma.

SUCCESS STORIES IN COMBATING STIGMA

Real-life examples highlight the progress made in challenging stigma:

Mental Health Advocacy Groups:
Initiatives like "Ending the Stigma" campaigns have successfully raised awareness and encouraged dialogue about BPD.

Therapeutic Innovations:
Increased availability of evidence-based therapies, such as Dialectical Behavior Therapy (DBT), has demonstrated that BPD is treatable, challenging notions of hopelessness.

Individual Advocacy:
People with BPD, like author and activist Marsha Linehan, have shared their journeys, inspiring hope and reducing stigma.

The stigma surrounding Borderline Personality Disorder is deeply entrenched, but it is not insurmountable. By addressing misconceptions through education, advocacy, and systemic change, we can

create a society that supports rather than ostracizes individuals with BPD.
Empathy, understanding, and informed action are key to breaking the cycle of stigma. When we challenge harmful stereotypes and amplify the voices of those with lived experience, we take crucial steps toward a world where individuals with BPD are treated with the dignity and respect they deserve.

CHAPTER 10

THE JOURNEY OF RECOVERY IN BORDERLINE PERSONALITY DISORDER: HOPE, HEALING, AND RESILIENCE

Recovery from Borderline Personality Disorder (BPD) is a complex and individualized process, often marked by both significant challenges and profound transformation. Unlike many other mental health conditions, BPD is frequently misunderstood and stigmatized, but with the right combination of therapy, self-awareness, and social support, individuals can experience healing and achieve a higher quality of life. This chapter will explore the journey of recovery from BPD, emphasizing the path to healing, the resilience required, and the hope for a better future.

UNDERSTANDING RECOVERY IN BPD

In the context of mental health, recovery does not necessarily mean a complete absence of symptoms. Instead, it refers to an ongoing process of personal growth, self-understanding, emotional regulation, and improved functionality. For those with BPD, recovery is not about "curing" the disorder but rather about learning to manage its symptoms and live a fulfilling life.

Recovery from BPD involves:

- **Emotional Regulation:**
Developing strategies to manage intense emotions and reduce emotional reactivity.
- Improved Relationships:
Strengthening interpersonal relationships by learning healthier communication and coping strategies.
- Self-Identity and Self-Awareness:
Establishing a stable sense of self, reducing feelings of emptiness, and improving self-esteem.

- Behavioral Change:
Recognizing and altering harmful behaviors like self-harm, impulsivity, or substance abuse.

It is important to acknowledge that recovery from BPD is not linear. There may be setbacks, relapses, or moments of doubt. However, individuals can build resilience and continue making progress by utilizing the tools they have learned in therapy and from their support networks.

THE ROLE OF THERAPY IN RECOVERY

The foundation of recovery from BPD lies in effective therapeutic interventions. One of the most widely recognized and evidence-based treatments for BPD is **Dialectical Behavior Therapy (DBT),** developed by Dr. Marsha Linehan in the 1980s. DBT has been shown to significantly reduce symptoms of BPD, including emotional dysregulation, suicidal ideation, and self-harming behaviors. It also focuses on building skills in four key areas:

1. Mindfulness:
Staying present in the moment and observing emotions without judgment.
2. Distress Tolerance:
Developing strategies to tolerate and cope with intense emotional experiences without resorting to harmful behaviors.
3. Emotion Regulation:
Identifying, understanding, and changing emotional responses to triggers.
4. Interpersonal Effectiveness:
Enhancing communication skills, setting boundaries, and building healthy relationships.

DBT has proven to be highly effective in helping individuals manage the emotional instability and interpersonal difficulties characteristic of BPD. By providing tools to handle extreme emotional states and navigate challenging relationships, DBT enables individuals to live more balanced and productive lives.

Other therapeutic approaches that contribute to recovery include **Cognitive Behavioral Therapy (CBT)**, which helps identify and reframe negative thought patterns, and **Mentalization-Based Therapy (MBT),** which helps individuals understand and interpret their own and others' behaviors and feelings. For some, **Schema Therapy** or **Transference-Focused Psychotherapy (TFP)** may also be beneficial in addressing deep-rooted issues related to identity and relationships.

BUILDING A STABLE SENSE OF SELF**

A hallmark of BPD is an unstable or fragmented sense of self, leading to feelings of emptiness, confusion, or self-loathing. In recovery, developing a more stable and coherent sense of identity is a critical goal. This often involves a process of self-discovery, self-compassion, and confronting the internalized beliefs that contribute to emotional pain.

EXPLORING IDENTITY IN RECOVERY

For many individuals with BPD, their sense of self is often influenced by the external world, including their relationships and social environments. This can lead to a sense of fluidity or uncertainty regarding their identity. Recovery involves grounding the individual in their internal sense of self understanding who they are, what they value, and what their true desires are.

Therapeutic interventions, such as DBT and MBT, often explore self-concept in depth. In DBT, for example, individuals learn to differentiate between "wise mind" (balanced emotional and rational thinking) and the extremes of emotional dysregulation or detachment from reality. As individuals practice mindfulness and develop emotional regulation skills, they become better able to align their behavior with their authentic values and needs.

It's also important to acknowledge that recovery may involve periods of self-exploration. Individuals may experiment with different aspects of their identity, such as career paths, social roles, or personal values, in order to define themselves more clearly.

RESILIENCE AND COPING SKILLS IN RECOVERY

Recovery from BPD requires immense resilience, as individuals must often confront years of emotional trauma, maladaptive behaviors, and intense feelings of shame or inadequacy. Resilience is the ability to bounce back from adversity, learn from setbacks, and continue progressing.

DEVELOPING HEALTHY COPING STRATEGIES

During the recovery process, individuals with BPD learn to replace maladaptive coping mechanisms such as self-harm, substance abuse, or impulsivity with healthier, more adaptive strategies. DBT teaches skills like **self-soothing**, **distraction techniques**, and **problem-solving,** all of which provide alternatives to harmful behaviors.

For instance, Sarah, a 27-year-old with BPD, used to cope with emotional pain through self-harm but gradually learned healthier alternatives, such as taking a walk, practicing deep breathing, or engaging in creative activities like painting. As Sarah built resilience, she became better equipped to handle emotional distress without resorting to harmful behaviors.

Additionally, **physical health** plays a crucial role in emotional well-being. Engaging in regular physical exercise, maintaining a balanced diet, and ensuring adequate sleep all contribute to emotional regulation and overall recovery.

RELATIONSHIPS IN RECOVERY

Interpersonal difficulties are central to BPD, and one of the key goals of recovery is to establish healthier, more stable relationships. This process involves not only learning new communication and relational skills but also addressing past trauma or attachment issues.

HEALTHY BOUNDARIES AND COMMUNICATION

In therapy, individuals with BPD learn the importance of setting healthy boundaries both in terms of protecting themselves from emotional harm and respecting the boundaries of others. DBT, for example, emphasizes the practice of **interpersonal effectiveness**, which teaches individuals how to communicate their needs assertively without resorting to manipulation or aggression.

For example, Mark, who struggled with BPD, learned to communicate his emotional needs clearly and respectfully with his partner, instead of relying on passive-aggressive behaviors or emotional outbursts. As a result, his relationships became more fulfilling, and his emotional stability improved.

REPAIRING RELATIONSHIPS WITH LOVED ONES

Recovery also involves repairing relationships that may have been strained due to BPD symptoms. Family therapy and couples counseling can be invaluable in addressing misunderstandings, improving communication, and teaching family members how to support their loved one in healthy ways.

In cases where relationships have been damaged beyond repair, individuals with BPD may also learn to grieve these losses and accept that some relationships may no longer serve their well-being. Therapy can help individuals process grief and let go of toxic relationships while building new, supportive connections.

CHALLENGES IN RECOVERY

While recovery is possible, it is often accompanied by challenges and setbacks. These can include:

- Relapse of Maladaptive Behaviors: During stressful periods, individuals may temporarily revert to unhealthy coping mechanisms, such as self-harm, impulsive spending, or substance abuse.

- Difficult Emotions and Trauma Triggers: Individuals with BPD may experience intense feelings of shame, guilt, or anger when they perceive themselves as failing or when they encounter situations that remind them of past trauma.

- Doubt and Fear of Abandonment:
The fear of abandonment, common in BPD, may persist even during recovery. Individuals may doubt whether others will remain supportive as they work through their emotional struggles.

It is important to acknowledge that these challenges do not signify failure in the recovery process. Instead, they are part of the journey. Having a strong support system, engaging in regular therapy, and practicing self-compassion can help individuals regain their footing after setbacks.

SUCCESS STORIES AND HOPE FOR THE FUTURE

There are countless success stories of individuals who have navigated the difficult journey of recovery from BPD and gone on to lead fulfilling lives. These stories offer hope and inspiration for others facing similar struggles.

Case Study: John's Recovery Journey
John, a 33-year-old man diagnosed with BPD, struggled with chronic emotional instability, difficulty maintaining relationships, and suicidal ideation. Through DBT and intensive individual therapy, he learned to regulate his emotions, set boundaries, and build healthier relationships. With time, John was able to reconcile with estranged family members, build a supportive network of friends, and pursue his career goals. Today, John is an advocate for BPD awareness and works to help others with similar struggles.

Such success stories demonstrate that recovery is possible with commitment, the right therapeutic support, and a belief in one's ability to change.

The journey of recovery from Borderline Personality Disorder is complex and often challenging, but it is also one filled with immense potential for growth and healing. With the right therapeutic tools, self-awareness, and social support, individuals with BPD can learn to manage their symptoms, build healthier relationships, and develop a more stable sense of self.

Recovery is not a linear process, but it is a journey that leads to hope, resilience, and the possibility of living a fulfilling life. By fostering understanding, empathy, and support, both individuals with BPD and the communities around them can create an environment in which healing is possible and the future is full of promise.

In embracing recovery, individuals with BPD demonstrate incredible strength and resilience, defying the stigma and challenges that have historically surrounded the disorder. Their journey offers inspiration to all who seek to overcome their own struggles, regardless of the obstacles they may face.

CONCLUSION

Throughout this book, we have explored the complexities of Borderline Personality Disorder (BPD), from its symptoms and causes to the stigma surrounding it and the path to recovery. BPD is a multifaceted condition, deeply affecting emotional regulation, self-identity, and interpersonal relationships. However, it is also a disorder that can be understood, managed, and overcome with the right tools, support, and resilience.

While the challenges faced by individuals with BPD are significant, they are not insurmountable. Recovery is not a linear process, but it is entirely possible. The key to healing lies in a comprehensive and compassionate approach one that combines effective therapeutic interventions, self-awareness, and social support. Tools such as Dialectical Behavior Therapy (DBT) and other therapeutic modalities offer individuals the opportunity to manage their emotional turbulence, build stable relationships, and cultivate a more balanced and fulfilling life.

An essential aspect of the journey of recovery is the dismantling of the stigma that surrounds BPD. Misunderstandings, misconceptions, and fear often lead to discrimination, making it harder for individuals to seek help and navigate their healing process. Yet, as we have seen, greater awareness and empathy can challenge these harmful stereotypes, creating a more supportive environment for those with BPD. Education, both within healthcare systems and broader society, is critical in changing perceptions and fostering an environment where individuals with BPD are seen for who they truly are not just their diagnosis.

The process of healing from BPD is marked by remarkable resilience. Individuals with

BPD, despite the emotional and interpersonal struggles they face, show incredible strength in their pursuit of better emotional health and personal growth. Their journey offers not just lessons in self-compassion, but also a powerful reminder of the importance of empathy, patience, and support from loved ones and communities.

In conclusion, Borderline Personality Disorder is a challenging yet treatable condition. It requires a nuanced understanding, a willingness to engage with the emotional experiences of those affected, and a commitment to breaking down the barriers of stigma and misunderstanding. With the right combination of therapeutic support, self-reflection, and community, individuals with BPD can experience profound growth, healing, and hope. Their stories of resilience and recovery offer a vision of a future where those with BPD can live fulfilling, meaningful lives, free from the weight of stigma and the limitations of their disorder.

The journey of recovery is not about perfection it is about progress, compassion, and the ability to create a life worth living. As we continue to learn more about BPD, its treatment, and its challenges, we must remember that every step toward understanding and healing is a victory, both for those with BPD and for society as a whole. Through ongoing education, open dialogue, and unwavering support, we can create a world where individuals with Borderline Personality Disorder are not defined by their struggles but empowered by their resilience and potential.

Printed in Great Britain
by Amazon